Harry Styles

By Linda Barghoorn

CRABTREE
PUBLISHING COMPANY
WWW.CRABTREEBOOKS.COM

WWW.CRABTREEBOOKS.COM

Author: Linda Barghoorn
Editor: Kathy Middleton
Proofreader: Lorna Notsch
Design, photo research, and prepress: Ken Wright
Print coordinator: Katherine Berti

Photo Credits
Alamy: title page, Wayne Howes;
p 5, ZUMA Press, Inc.; pp 7, 9, 11, 12, 14, 17, 18, WENN Ltd; p 8, brinkstock; p10, DWD-Media; p 13m Bob Rendtorff; p 15, Photo 12; pp 16, 19, EDB Image Archive; p 22, INTERFOTO; pp 23, 28 PA Images; p 25, United Archives GmbH; p2\ 26, Rich Gold
Getty: p 6, David M. Benett; p 20, Gilbert Carrasquillo; p 21, David Krieger/Bauer-Griffin; p 24, Kevin Mazur
Keystone: Cover, © PS3; p 27, © Starmax
Wikimedia: p 4, Sepideh (Sepi)

Every effort has been made to trace copyright holders and to obtain their permission for use of copyright material. The authors and publishers would be pleased to rectify any error or omission in future editions. All the Internet addresses given in this book were correct at the time of going to press. The author and publishers regret any inconvenience caused if addresses have changed or sites have ceased to exist, but can accept no responsibility for any such changes.

Library and Archives Canada Cataloguing in Publication

Barghoorn, Linda, author
    Harry Styles / Linda Barghoorn.

(Superstars!)
Includes index.
Issued in print and electronic formats.
ISBN 978-0-7787-4833-5 (hardcover).--
ISBN 978-0-7787-4848-9 (softcover).--
ISBN 978-1-4271-2096-0 (HTML)

    1. Styles, Harry, 1994- --Juvenile literature. 2. Singers--England--Biography--Juvenile literature. I. Title. II. Series: Superstars! (St. Catharines, Ont.)

ML3930.S938B25 2018   j782.42164092   C2018-900279-4
                                                                             C2018-900280-8

Library of Congress Cataloging-in-Publication Data

Names: Barghoorn, Linda, author.
Title: Harry Styles / Linda Barghoorn.
Description: New York, New York : Crabtree Publishing Company, 2018. | Series: Superstars! | Includes index.
Identifiers: LCCN 2018005820 (print) |
  LCCN 2018006383 (ebook) |
  ISBN 9781427120960 (Electronic) |
  ISBN 9780778748335 (hardcover) |
  ISBN 9780778748489 (pbk.)
Subjects: LCSH: Styles, Harry, 1994---Juvenile literature. | Singers--England--Biography--Juvenile literature.
Classification: LCC ML3930.S89 (ebook) | LCC ML3930.S89 B37 2018 (print) | DDC 782.42166092 [B] --dc23
LC record available at https://lccn.loc.gov/2018005820

Crabtree Publishing Company

Printed in the U.S.A./052018/BG20180327

www.crabtreebooks.com   1-800-387-7650
Copyright © 2018 CRABTREE PUBLISHING COMPANY. All rights reserved. No part of this publication may be reproduced, stored in a retrieval system or be transmitted in any form or by any means, electronic, mechanical, photocopying, recording, or otherwise, without the prior written permission of Crabtree Publishing Company. In Canada: We acknowledge the financial supportof the Government of Canada through the Canada Book Fund for our publishing activities.

Published in Canada
Crabtree Publishing
616 Welland Ave.
St. Catharines, ON
L2M 5V6

Published in the United States
Crabtree Publishing
PMB 59051
350 Fifth Avenue, 59th Floor
New York, New York 10118

Published in the United Kingdom
Crabtree Publishing
Maritime House
Basin Road North, Hove
BN41 1WR

Published in Australia
Crabtree Publishing
3 Charles Street
Coburg North
VIC 3058

CONTENTS

Just Like Any Other 4

Taking the Lead 8

A New Boy Band 12

Five Albums, Four Tours 18

What's Next? 28

Timeline 29

Glossary 30

Find Out More 31

Index 32

Words that are defined in the glossary are in
bold type the first time they appear in the text.

Just Like Any Other

Harry Styles was like any other teenage boy growing up in a small town in England. He attended high school, performed with friends in a local band, dated girls, and worked part-time to earn spending money. But his life changed forever when he entered a singing competition on the British talent-seeking show, *The X Factor*.

Harry was just 16 years old when he **auditioned** for *The X Factor*.

Meet H
Harry is known as "H" or "Hazza" to his friends and fans.

Rising Star

No one—including Harry—could have imagined what would come next! Within only a few months of entering the competition, Harry found himself in the finals as part of a five-member group that called itself One Direction. When the competition ended, the boys set out on a fast-paced tour of England, performing in stadiums packed with thousands of fans. Harry and his four bandmates skyrocketed to fame. They would ultimately become one of the biggest boy bands of all time.

In the Spotlight

Charming, handsome, and funny, Harry is super popular. But, life as a superstar comes with intense, up-close attention by both the **paparazzi** and adoring fans. Every part of Harry's life—from his changing hairstyles to his flashy clothes, his relationships, his collection of tattoos, and his song lyrics—is watched closely.

Harry has grown up in the spotlight.

Striking out on His Own

When One Direction announced the bandmates were taking a break after five years at the top of the charts, their fans were crushed. But Harry grabbed the chance to explore new ways to express himself as an artist, actor, and solo singer. Although his initial success on the music scene seemed almost accidental, this superstar is here to stay!

" She Said It "

"We never dreamed things would go the way they did. He has just kept on winning and winning."
—Gemma Styles, *The Sun*, September 2016

A Love for Music

Harry Edward Styles was born on February 1, 1994. He grew up in the small town of Holmes Chapel in Cheshire County, northern England. When asked what it's like there, Harry has joked that "it's quite boring; nothing much happens there." His parents—Desmond Styles and Anne Twist—divorced when he was seven, but he remained close with both parents. Harry lived with his mom and his older sister, Gemma. She was a devoted and hard-working student. Harry, on the other hand, loved to play jokes and clown around. He was sometimes jealous of his sister's successes at school.

Harry and his sister Gemma Styles attend the Another Man A/W launch event in 2016.

Harry grew up surrounded by music, and he learned to appreciate a wide range of musical styles. His father was a fan of classic rock bands such as the Rolling Stones, Fleetwood Mac, and Pink Floyd. His mother enjoyed pop artists such as Shania Twain and Norah Jones. Harry says the artists whose music influenced him the most were Elvis Presley and Freddie Mercury, the lead singer of the rock band Queen.

Popular and Funny

As a teenager, Harry was popular and funny. He enjoyed hanging out with his friends and chatting up girls at Holmes Chapel Comprehensive School, where he attended high school. On Saturdays, Harry worked at the town bakery with his best friend, Nick Clough. Always polite and helpful, Harry was as popular with the shop's customers as he was at school. He and Nick earned just enough to pay for Saturday nights out in the lively city of Manchester, less than an hour away. At the time, he earned about $8 an hour—quite a bit less than he would go on to make as a global pop superstar!

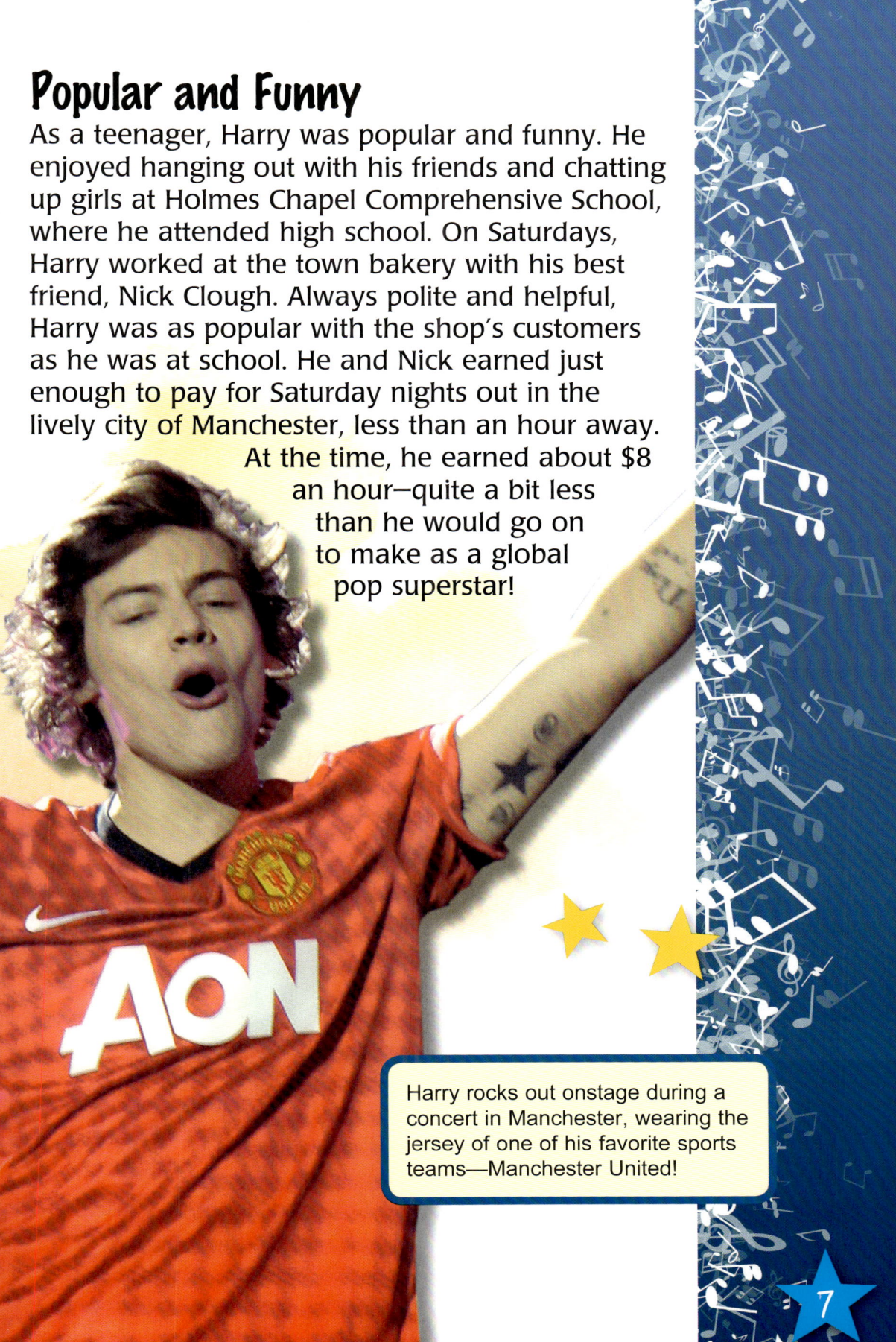

Harry rocks out onstage during a concert in Manchester, wearing the jersey of one of his favorite sports teams—Manchester United!

Taking the Lead

Nick and Harry formed a punk-pop band in high school. Their friends Hayden Morris and Will Sweeney joined the group, which they called White Eskimo. Hayden played rhythm guitar, while Will played drums. Nick took up his position as the bass guitarist after convincing Harry to give up the bass to sing lead vocals. While Harry had always loved to sing in private, he wasn't confident about his actual singing abilities. But being the easygoing teenager that he was, Harry agreed to give it a try.

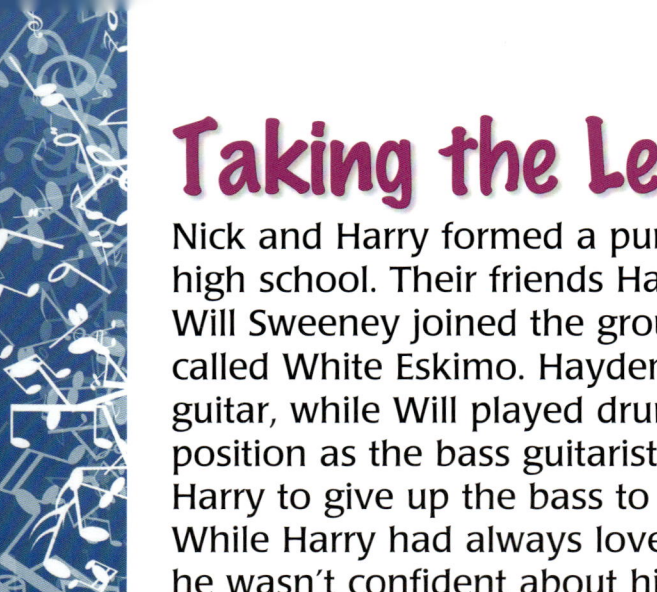

The bakery in Holmes Chapel is a popular spot for Harry's fans to visit.

Backroom Performance

One day at the bakery, Harry was cleaning in the back room. Assuming no one was listening, he began singing at the top of his voice while sweeping. When some customers came in and heard him, they wanted to know if he had ever considered singing professionally. They suggested that he call them if he ever decided to try.

A Passion for Performing

The band performed at various **venues** around town and even won a local Battle of the Bands competition. As his band began to build a fan base, Harry gained confidence and developed a real passion for performing live. Most of the material the band performed were **covers** of other artists' songs. He performed with the band for seven months before graduating from high school and leaving to audition for *The X Factor*. His bandmates—who are still together today, often joke that Harry is still a band member, because he never officially told them that he was quitting!

Harry arriving at Fountain Studios for *X-Factor* rehearsals.

"I got such a thrill when I was in front of people singing, it made me want to do it more and more."
—Harry Styles, *The X Factor*, April 2010

The X Factor

Harry exploded onto the British music scene when he auditioned for *The X Factor* in 2010. He had decided to audition for the British music competition after his mother suggested he try out. He laughs when he remembers her absolute confidence in his talent. Mothers—he suggests—always believe in their children's extraordinary talents, even when they may not exist. Although Harry wasn't as confident, he tried out anyway. He was eager to get honest feedback about whether he really had talent. In April, 16-year-old Harry traveled with his family to the tryouts in Manchester. Sporting T-shirts printed with the proud claim, "We think Harry has the X factor," his nervous family waited and watched backstage as Harry took his place in front of the microphone.

The X Factor began as a British television show. It features competitions to find new singing talents among solo and group performers.

Meet the Judges

There were three music industry professionals judging the competition. Simon Cowell is an accomplished British music producer. Nicole Scherzinger is an American singer and actor who rose to fame while part of the successful Pussycat Dolls band. Louis Walsh is an Irish entertainment manager who helped create the bands Boyzone and Westlife. Each judge knew a lot about the music business and what it takes to be successful.

Round One

Harry had chosen to sing Stevie Wonder's song, "Isn't She Lovely." He seemed relaxed and confident as he sang **a cappella**. When he finished, the crowd erupted into cheers and loud applause. Now all that was left was for the judges to announce their decision. Would Harry advance to the next stage of the competition or be sent home? While Louis felt Harry lacked the experience to move forward, Simon and Nicole saw talent and potential in his performance. With a vote of 2:1, Harry advanced to the next round.

Simon Cowell (center right) saw potential in Harry during his audition.

"I think with a bit of vocal coaching you actually could be very good."
—Simon Cowell, *The X Factor*, April 2010

A New Boy Band

As the competition continued, Harry was cut from the solo competition. So were four other boys who the judges felt were talented but not strong enough to continue as individual performers. Nicole Scherzinger suggested putting the five boys together to compete in the group competition. Harry was introduced to Niall Horan, Zayn Malik, Liam Payne, and Louis Tomlinson. They were excited at the chance to stay in the competition and agreed to form their own group.

The boys of 1D were only teenagers when they met on *The X Factor*.

What's in a Name?

The boys needed to choose a name for their group before the next round of competition began. The band members tossed around many suggestions. Some were silly, others were embarrassing. Just when it seemed like they might never agree, Harry came up with an idea. He knew that all five bandmates would have to follow "one direction" to be successful, and he believed the name would sound cool when they were introduced. The others agreed, and One Direction was officially born.

The Group Competition

The boys met often during the next few weeks to get to know one another, to practice singing, and to develop their sound as a group. Being teenagers, they enjoyed joking around and having fun. But the boys also worked hard, pursuing their music with passion and enthusiasm. In October, the show's group competition began in London. One Direction had decided to perform the song "Vida la Vida" by the British band Coldplay. Although they finished fourth on the first night of competition, Simon Cowell praised their performance. He called them confident, fun, and fearless. He'd seen them combine their talents into a group that was coming together like old friends. One of the other judges called the boys "five **heartthrobs**." Harry's talent and ability to charm the crowd was obvious. During these early performances, he began to emerge as the group's **front man**.

Simon Cowell saw talent in the boys of 1D.

" He Said It "

"His charming personal and elastic vocals had him positioned as the Timberlake of the group."
—Tim Sendra, *AllMusic* review, May 12, 2017

Soaring Popularity

As each week passed, One Direction drew more fans and more praise from the judges. Their popularity soared as they performed a wide variety of songs by artists ranging from The Beatles to Snow Patrol and Bryan Adams. Viewers tuned in across the country to watch the group perform and cast their votes in support of them.

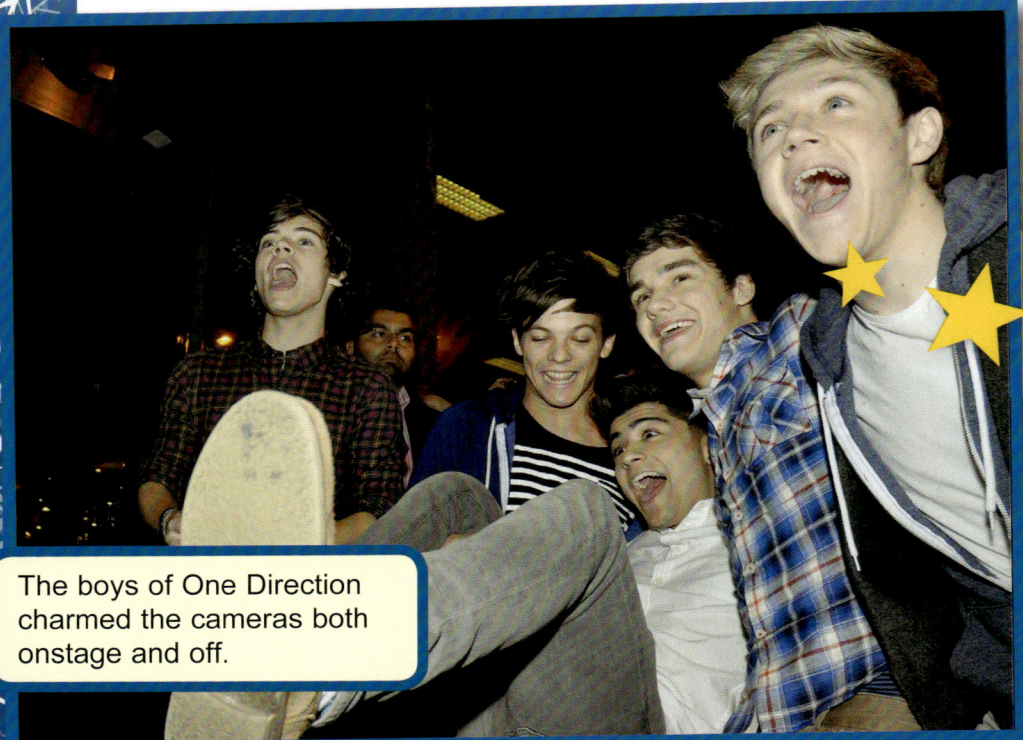

The boys of One Direction charmed the cameras both onstage and off.

Surviving the Competition

One Direction finished in third or fourth place each show, avoiding elimination for nine weeks. It was exciting and stressful, high-energy and exhausting. By Week 10—the final round of the competition—they were still in the running. This made them the first-ever **manufactured** singing group—a group created out of solo artists—to make it all the way to the finals. For their final performance, they chose to sing an **acoustic** version of Natalie Imbruglia's song "Torn."

Eliminated!

With their last performance of the competition behind them, they waited for the judges' decision. After two rounds of judging, they were in third place. But only two winners would be announced. As the final minutes of the competition ticked by, One Direction was eliminated. Five boys who had been unsuccessful in the individual competition had had a second chance at success. Although they had not won, who could have guessed that they were about to become one of the most successful boy bands on the planet—ever?

" He Said It "

"The band changed my life, gave me everything."
—Harry Styles, *Rolling Stone*, April 2017

On the Road

In February 2011, One Direction and other *X Factor* contestants set off on an X Factor Live tour across England and Ireland. They performed in front of more than 500,000 people in 13 cities over 10 weeks. Screaming teenage fans turned up to see One Direction. Harry—the youngest and most outgoing member of the band—soon had fans numbering in the thousands!

A Recording Contract

After that, things began to happen really fast! As the tour wrapped up, the boys needed to decide what to do next. Simon Cowell, the judge who had **mentored** the boys, also owned a music entertainment company. He offered One Direction a recording contract. The contract was estimated to be worth $2.5 million—more money than any of the teenage boys could ever have imagined earning.

No Way!
One Direction was sometimes called 1D. The group's fans were nicknamed "Directioners."

The media snapped pictures of Harry both onstage and off, including while out shopping.

Spotlight on Stardom

Five boys who had just met were now an official band with a recording contract. Their music careers were taking off at a speed they sometimes had a hard time keeping up with. Success, fortune, and stardom would put many pressures on them as teenagers and band members. As the band's youngest member, Harry was forced to grow up quickly under the bright lights and intense attention that came with pop stardom. Every aspect of his life—public and private—was **scrutinized** by his fans and the media.

Up All Night

The band's first album was called *Up All Night*. They recorded it in three studios: in Stockholm, Sweden; London, England, and Los Angeles, California. The boys worked with a number of different producers as they experimented with the sound and style they wanted to showcase on their **debut** album. Songwriters Ed Sheeran and Kelly Clarkson, among others, contributed songs for the album.

Up All Night was released in November 2011

Brit Pop

One Direction set a Guinness World Record when they became the first British group to land at number one on the US charts with their debut album.

Topping the Charts

When the album was released it quickly reached number two on the British music charts and number one in the United States. It sold more than 4.5 million copies around the world and skyrocketed to number one in 16 countries. The album featured four hit singles, including "What Makes You Beautiful," which debuted at number one on the British Singles Chart.

Five Albums, Four Tours

As their hits piled up, the band announced their first world tour. Tickets for the English cities on the tour sold out in an incredible 12 minutes! Directioners couldn't wait to see the boys perform live. Harry and his bandmates set out on a 12-month tour, performing 60 shows across the globe. With the success of the first tour, others soon followed. Between 2012 and 2015, there was little time to rest. The boys continued to produce albums and fill concert halls on tour. Their demanding tour schedule saw them complete four world tours in four years. They performed more than 380 concerts and traveled for more than 122 weeks. That's more than two full years on tour—away from family, friends, and everyday life! Between tours, One Direction recorded four more albums, releasing one album each year. Their status as pop stars was sealed. Harry couldn't imagine doing anything else.

Harry connects with the crowd at a packed stadium in Gothenburg, Sweden.

" He Said It "

"I'm 100 percent in this band. I still want to be touring with One Direction in 10 years. I'll be doing it until I'm old, and people are telling me to stop."
—*One Direction: This Is Us*, August 2013

Fashion Flare

The boys grew up in front of their fans as the band grew in popularity and **commercial** success. As they matured from teenagers into young men, each member cultivated his own style as a pop star. But Harry—more than all the others—developed a sense of style and fashion that was uniquely his. He left behind the preppy **chinos** and T-shirts that he had favored during his mid-teens. Instead, he enjoyed wearing bold and flamboyant clothes at concerts and celebrity events—proudly showing off pink frills, outrageous prints, slimmed-down tuxedos, and flashy boots. In 2013, the British public showed its appreciation of Harry's style by casting their votes in support of Harry to win a British Fashion Award. A few years later, Harry was ranked number six in *British GQ*'s list of best-dressed men of 2016.

Styles' Style

Harry has sported many styles, featuring everything from silk tuxedos to skinny jeans. He enjoys designer fashion, especially Saint Laurent, Burberry, and Gucci, but still loves to relax in jeans or slouchy sweatpants.

Heartthrob Harry rocked a tuxedo jacket at the Soho House private members' club in London in 2013.

Inked

Harry's tattoo collection has grown along with his love of fashion. From the time he was small, he liked to experiment with designs. His friend from the bakery—Nick Clough—remembers the pretend tattoos Harry liked to draw on himself as a young teen. Since then, Harry has used his body as a canvas for a growing collection of real tattoos: from butterflies and birdcages to initials and skeletons. These tattoos—like everything in Harry's personal life—are analyzed in great detail by fans and the paparazzi. It is as if they hold the key to understanding the man behind the music.

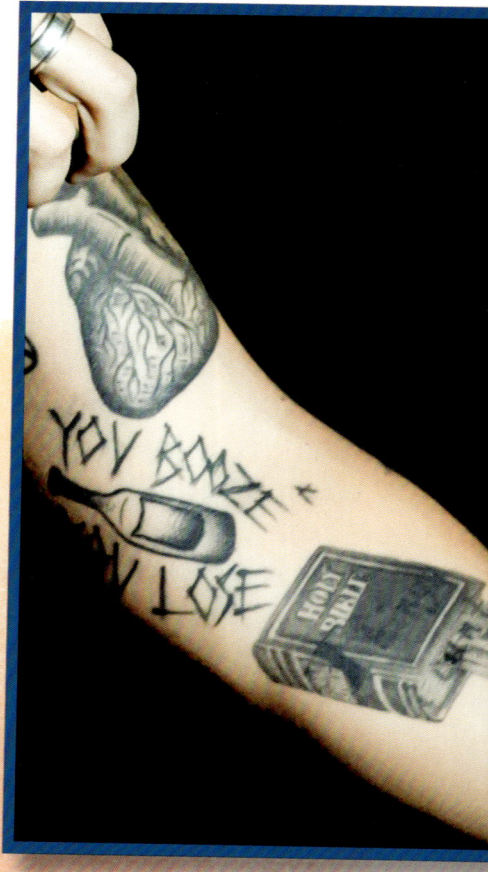

Harry refuses to reveal much about how many tattoos he has or what they mean. While he remains silent, those who know him suggest he has more than 60 tattoos! Exchanging theories on what each of them means has become like a celebrity sport for Harry's fans.

" He Said It "

"It's funny, because when we were younger and saw ourselves as rockers, I suggested we get our ears pierced. He was worried what his mum would think."
—Nick Clough, LiveJournal, April 2013

Public and Private

Harry's talent, outgoing personality, and good looks have earned him millions of fans around the world who follow his life closely on social media. Harry works hard to protect his privacy. He prefers to remain mysterious and secretive about his personal life and relationships. He has become as talented at dodging personal interview questions as he has at performing. It's hard work dating and sharing time with friends when you are as famous as Harry. While media and fans have **speculated** about his relationships, Harry has admitted very little. Even his most famous relationship, with Taylor Swift in 2012, remained mysterious and vague. It ended in public as quietly as it had begun—with no explanations and no announcements. Instead, Taylor and Harry seemed to prefer to let their songs speak for them.

Swift Song

Fans think the **lyrics** from One Direction's song "Perfect" are about Taylor Swift, who is known for her songs about relationships and breakups: "If you're looking for someone to write your breakup songs about, baby, I'm perfect."

Harry and Taylor's high-profile relationship lasted only a few months.

The Band Breaks Up

In March 2015, Zayn left 1D. Later that year, One Direction announced they were taking a break. After five years of hit singles and sold-out shows, the boys wanted to pursue individual music projects. They reassured anxious fans that they were not breaking up. But this news was short-lived. In January 2016, the band announced they were parting ways for good. They had sold more than 70 million records, reached number one on the charts 137 times, and won many music and video awards. It was time to move on—in a new direction.

Now a four-man band, 1D pose at the 2015 American Music Awards.

Going Solo

Harry began to consider what a solo career might look like. As a member of a band, he had never had the opportunity to explore a style of music that was uniquely his own. He was excited to write songs that allowed him to express ideas that were important to him—such as equal rights, love, and relationships. He wanted to share his own personal stories with his fans.

Debut Album

Harry signed a recording deal and organized a group of musicians to help him record his first solo album. Many of these musicians made their debut on this album. In fact, guitarist Mitch Rowland was recruited from a pizza shop when the original guitarist had to miss one of the recording sessions. Harry wrote all the songs for the album, but refuses to discuss the meaning of his lyrics. He leaves that for his fans to figure out. Free to chart his own path, Harry seemed less concerned with writing hit songs than with writing about what was important to him. And it worked! His debut album, *Harry Styles*, received many positive reviews. His first single—"Sign of the Times"—reached number one in more than 55 countries.

Real Player

Harry has cowritten songs with Snow Patrol's Johnny McDaid and solo artist Meghan Trainor. He has also written songs for Michael Bublé and Ariana Grande. Besides singing, he can play guitar, piano, and drums.

As a solo artist, Harry presented an entirely new sound to his millions of fans.

" He Said It "

"I've never felt this vulnerable putting out music, because I don't think this is a piece of myself I've put out there before." —NPR, June 2, 2017

A Sense of Humor...

Despite the pressures of stardom, Harry tries not to take life too seriously. Among his friends and family, Harry is well-known for his sense of humor and love of practical jokes. In a *Saturday Night Live* (SNL) skit, Harry performed a hilarious **impersonation** of Mick Jagger from the Rolling Stones. His performance earned Harry praise from Mick, who claimed it was one of the best impersonations of him ever. Harry also appeared with his friend, comedian James Corden, in another comedy skit in which two characters can't stop singing, even when faced with incredibly serious situations. The results are sidesplittingly funny.

Harry impersonated Mick Jagger on a game show during his SNL appearance.

...And a Passion for Art

As a young adult, Harry developed a passion for modern art. He owns a small personal collection of paintings, sculptures, and **taxidermy** by some of England's edgiest artists. Harry's dream is to have Bambi—a London **street artist**—paint a mural in his home. But that's not likely to happen anytime soon. Although her work can be found in streets around London, she has refused to let anyone know who she really is!

Harry the Philanthropist

Harry calls himself a **feminist**. He supports equal rights for everyone. He has used his fame to bring attention to many important causes. While he was a member of One Direction, Harry joined bandmate Liam Payne to support a British cancer charity called Trekstock. Together, they helped raise more than $750,000 for cancer research to help young adults. On the band's 2015 world tour, Harry visited a project in Cape Town, South Africa, where he met with children suffering from poverty and conflict. He has also supported Little Princess Trust, a charity in England that provides wigs to boys and girls who have lost their hair because of cancer. Harry's social media post showing him cutting off a braid of his hair received more than one million "likes" and helped raise awareness about the charity and its important work.

Pop Art

Harry's most important art purchase was a painting by the late Jean-Michel Basquiat, a famous American graffiti artist from New York City.

" They Said It "

"He is an avid collector and has a seriously impressive gallery worth millions of pounds in his house."
—Anonymous source, *The Sun*, January 21, 2016

On the Big Screen

Harry made his acting debut in the movie *Dunkirk*, one of the most talked about and successful movies of 2017. It told the story of the **evacuation** of thousands of British soldiers from the beaches of northern France during World War II. Harry—despite his celebrity status—auditioned alongside hundreds of other actors for the part of Alex, one of the British soldiers. When Harry got the part, the movie's director, Christopher Nolan, insisted that his fame from One Direction had nothing to do with him being cast in the movie. He says Harry totally earned the role. The singer showed a real talent for acting and had the right look to play a character who lived in that era of history. Harry also worked hard to downplay his role as a pop star and was keen to work with and support the other actors as an equal member of the cast. The result was a performance that has been widely applauded by movie critics. At the movie's premiere in London, Harry spoke excitedly about the experience. Could this be the beginning of a move in a new career direction?

Harry poses on the red carpet at the London premiere of *Dunkirk* in July 2017.

" He Said It "

"I just feel very lucky to have been able to work with such an amazing group of actors. It's been a lot of fun. I feel very fortunate."
—*The Sun*, January 21, 2016

His Best Year Yet

The year 2017 was another exciting time for Harry as he continued to collect awards and praise for his solo work. The Teen Choice Awards honored him with awards for Male Artist, Breakout Movie Star, and Best Song. He also received MTV Music Awards for Best Pop Video and Visual Effects for "Sign of the Times." He is now widely recognized as a style icon. Magazines such as *Rolling Stone* (USA) and *The Sunday Times* (UK) celebrated his style by featuring him on their covers. Harry's fame has continued to grow as he explores opportunities to showcase his talents on concert stages, movie screens, and music albums. He marked another milestone in September 2017, when he set out on his first solo world tour. His fans were eager to see him back on stage—tickets sold out in less than 30 seconds!

Harry rocks out in the streets of New York City during an appearance on the *TODAY* show in 2017.

What's Next?

Harry's life is always hectic as he juggles his time among recording music, touring, and acting. While he owns homes in New York and Los Angeles, his favorite place is still London, where he feels he can be himself. He continues to be close to his family and loves spending time at his mom's home in England. It's a quiet place to relax and escape from the spotlight. A lot has happened to Harry since he left his hometown of Holmes Chapel to try his luck at a music career. Even Harry couldn't have imagined the life and success he is enjoying today as one of the most famous pop stars on the planet. The sky seems to be the limit for Harry Styles! Few people doubt that he will be successful in whatever direction he chooses.

❝ He Said It ❞

"I'm trying to enjoy the moment and not be pressured too much."
—Harry Styles, *The Sun*, May 2017

Timeline

1994: Harry Edward Styles is born in Redditch, England, on February 1st

2010: Harry auditions as a solo candidate for *The X Factor* in Manchester. Unsuccessful in his bid as a solo performer, Harry joins four other teenage boys to form One Direction.

2011: After placing third in the competition, One Direction takes part in the X Factor Live tour, performing for more than 500,000 fans

2011: One Direction releases their first album and announces a six-month world tour across 46 cities for which tickets sell out in minutes

2012: One Direction performs at the 2012 Olympics Closing Ceremony in London, England

2013: The band's second world tour covers 70 cities, spending most of the year on the road away from friends and family

2015: One Direction announces they are taking a break to pursue individual music projects

2015: The band's last album is released. It is their fifth album to debut in the Top 10, breaking a record previously set by The Beatles

2016: One Direction announces they are breaking up for good. Harry sets out on a solo music career.

2016: Harry signs a three-album recording deal with Columbia Records

2017: Harry celebrates his 23rd birthday at a posh private party in California with many famous guests, including Adele

2017: Harry's self-titled debut album, *Harry Styles*, is released and debuts at number one in the United States, England, and Australia and his first single, "Sign of the Times," quickly climbs the charts

2017: Harry makes his acting debut as a World War II soldier in *Dunkirk*

2017: Harry begins his first world tour as a solo artist, *Harry Styles: Live on Tour*, in San Francisco in September

Glossary

a capella Singing without any musical accompaniment
acoustic Music that does not have its sound changed by electronic devices
audition A short performance to display the talent of a performer
chinos Casual pants made of a stiff fabric that are usually light brown in color
commercial Viewed with regard to profit
cover A new version of a song by someone other than the original artist or composer
debut The first public performance or appearance
evacuation Removal from a dangerous place
feminist Someone who supports women's rights and interests
front man The lead singer of a pop or rock group
heartthrob An attractive man or woman who is often famous
impersonation Pretending to be someone else
lyrics The words of a song
manufacture To make up from existing parts
mentor To act as a teacher or give advice to a less experienced person
paparazzi Photographers who follow famous people to take photos, which they sell to the media
scrutinize To examine something in great detail
speculate To think about something and make guesses about it
street artist Someone who creates visual art in public places that are not traditional art venues
taxidermy Preparing, stuffing, and mounting animal skins
venue Where an event takes place

Find Out More

Books

Croft, Malcom. *Harry Styles: Evolution of a Modern Superstar.* Carlton, 2018.

Cronin, Ali. *Harry Styles: The Biography, Offstage.* Penguin Workshop, 2017.

Peppas, Lynn. *One Direction.* Crabtree, 2013.

Websites

Billboard: Harry Styles Career Highlights
www.billboard.com/articles/columns/pop/7743599/harry-styles-career-highlights-timeline

Harry Styles Official Website:
www.hstyles.co.uk

Index

albums
　Harry Styles 23
　Up All Night 17
awards 19, 27
Bambi 24
Basquiat, Jean-Michel 25
Clough, Nick 7, 8, 20
Corden, James 24
Cowell, Simon 10, 11, 13, 16
Directioners 16, 18
Dunkirk 26
family 5, 6, 28
Fleetwood Mac 6
Guinness World Record 17
Horan, Niall 12, 13, 14, 15, 16, 17, 18, 19, 22
Holmes Chapel Comprehensive School 7
Jagger, Mick 24
Jones, Norah 6
Little Princess Trust 25
Malik, Zayn 12, 13, 14, 15, 16, 17, 18, 19, 22
Manchester United 7
Mercury, Freddie 6
Morris, Hayden 8
One Direction 4, 5, 12, 13, 14, 15, 16, 17, 18, 19, 21, 22, 25
Payne, Liam 12, 13, 14, 15, 16, 17, 18, 19, 22, 25
Pink Floyd 6
Presley, Elvis 6
Rolling Stones 6, 24
Rowland, Mitch 23
Saturday Night Live 24
Scherzinger, Nicole 10, 11, 12
songs
　"Perfect" 21
　"Sign of the Times" 23, 27
　"What Makes You Beautiful" 17
Sweeney, Will 8
Swift, Taylor 21
tattoos 5, 20
Trekstock 25
TODAY 27
Tomlinson, Louis 12, 13, 14, 15, 16, 17, 18, 19, 22
Twain, Shania 6
Walsh, Louis 10, 11
White Eskimo 8, 9
X Factor 4, 9, 10, 11, 12, 13, 14, 15

About the Author

Linda Barghoorn has been sharing stories—hers and others—for years. She has interviewed rap musicians, TV news anchors, and most importantly, her dad. She is the author of 20 children's books and is writing a novel about her father's life.